CW00735942

Index:

20 Practical Advises — 3-6

Basic recipes — 8-13

Appetizers — 15-25

Pasta and Risotto — 27-55

Main Courses — 57-99

Pizza — 101-108

Side Dishes — 110-128

Dessert — 130-142

20 Consigli Pratici

20 Pratical Advices

1. **Quality of Ingredients:** Always use fresh, high-quality ingredients. Italians place high value on the freshness and quality of their ingredients.

2. **Water for Pasta:** Ensure the water is boiling before adding pasta. Also, add a handful of salt to season the pasta.

3. **Don't Drain Everything:** When draining the pasta, always save some of the cooking water to adjust the consistency of the sauce.

4. **Cooking Pasta:** Cook the pasta until it is al dente. It should be fully cooked but still firm to the bite.

5. **Garlic and Onion:** Do not burn the garlic and onion when sautéing, as they will become bitter.

6. **Fresh Herbs:** Enhance your dishes with fresh herbs such as basil, rosemary, and sage for added flavor.

7. **Use of Wine:** Wine is often used in Italian cooking. Be sure to use a good-quality wine that you would enjoy drinking on its own.

8. **Time and Patience:** Take your time to cook and savor your dishes. Italian cooking is about more than nutrition; it is also about enjoying the process and the experience.

9. **Room Temperature Ingredients:** Use ingredients at room temperature for desserts like ciambellone to achieve a uniform consistency and prevent the dessert from deflating.

10. **Measure the Ingredients:** While Italians often don't use measuring cups, those new to Italian cooking might find accurately measuring ingredients helpful.

11. **Working the Flour:** When preparing dough, work the flour as little as possible to prevent developing too much gluten, which can result in a dessert or pasta that is too elastic or chewy.

12. **Powdered Sugar for Decorating:** Decorate desserts with powdered sugar rather than granulated sugar for a more refined appearance and better texture.

13. **Fresh Yeast vs. Baking Powder:** Be aware of the differences between fresh yeast and baking powder. They are not always interchangeable in recipes.

14. **Resting the Dough:** Allow doughs, especially pizza dough, to rest to enable the formation of air bubbles and to achieve a light and crispy texture.

15. **Use of Salt:** Season dishes carefully to balance flavors. Salt is crucial for enhancing flavor.

16. **Creaming Risottos:** To create a creamy texture, finish cooking risottos by stirring in butter and Parmigiano Reggiano.

17. **Cooking Fish:** Avoid overcooking fish; it is often best when slightly moist inside.

18. **Cooling Desserts:** Allow desserts to cool completely before cutting to prevent them from crumbling.

19. **Extra Virgin Olive Oil:** Flavor raw dishes with extra virgin olive oil, but consider using a less expensive olive oil for cooking.

20. **Love:** Last but not least, always cook with love!

Ricette Base

"Basic recipes"

Pane Fatto in Casa

Homemade Bread

SERVINGS: 2   PREPPING TIME: 2-3 HOURS   COOKING TIME: 30 MIN

INGREDIENTS

500g of type oo flour (or bread flour)

325ml of lukewarm water

10g of salt

7g of dry yeast (or 15g of fresh yeast)

One tablespoon of olive oil (optional)

DIRECTIONS

1. In a large bowl, mix the flour and salt.
2. In a glass, mix the yeast in the lukewarm water and let it sit for a few minutes.
3. Slowly pour the liquid into the bowl with the flour, mixing with a fork or hands until a dough forms.
4. Add the olive oil, if desired, for extra flavor.
5. Transfer the dough to a floured surface and knead it for about 10 minutes, until it becomes smooth and elastic.
6. Place the dough in an oil-greased bowl, cover it with a damp cloth, and let it rise in a warm place for about 1-2 hours, or until it doubles in volume.
7. Preheat the oven to 220°C, shape the dough on a floured surface, and let it rise on a baking tray for another 30 minutes. After making cuts on its surface, bake the bread until golden, around 30 minutes, then cool completely before slicing.

Pasta Sfoglia

Puff Pastry

SERVINGS: 2   PREPPING TIME: 3-4 HOURS   COOKING TIME: 20 MIN

INGREDIENTS

250 g of oo Flour
250 g of Butter (cold)
125 ml of Water (cold)
A pinch of Salt

DIRECTIONS

Base Dough Preparation:**

1. – Mix flour and salt, add cold water to form dough, wrap and refrigerate for 30 minutes.
2. Butter Preparation: Flatten cold butter between parchment sheets and refrigerate.
3. Laminating: Roll dough into a rectangle, place butter in the center, fold and seal edges. Roll and fold into thirds, refrigerate for 20 minutes.
4. Repeating Folds: Repeat laminating process for 5 more folds, resting dough in the refrigerator between each.
5. Final Rest: After the last fold, wrap and refrigerate puff pastry for at least 1 hour before using.

IMPASTO PIZZA

Pizza dough

SERVINGS: 2   PREPPING TIME: 15 MIN   COOKING TIME: 15 MIN

INGREDIENTS

500g (4 cups) all-purpose
flour

1 tsp sugar

1 tbsp salt

1 tbsp olive oil

1 packet (7g) active dry
yeast

325ml (1 1/3 cups) warm
water (approximately 40–
45°C or 105-110°F)

DIRECTIONS

1. Combine warm water and sugar in a bowl, then sprinkle yeast on top. Allow to sit for 5 minutes until it foams.
2. In a large bowl, mix flour and salt. Create a well in the center, adding the yeast mixture and olive oil.
3. Knead the resulting dough on a floured surface for about 10 minutes until smooth.
4. Place dough in an oiled bowl, covering it, and let it rise until it doubles in size (1.5-2 hours).
5. Once risen, punch the dough down, divide it into equal pieces, shape into balls, and let rest for another 30 minutes.
6. Roll out the dough on a floured surface to your desired thickness, ready for toppings.
7. Preheat the oven to its highest setting (220-250°C or 425-480°F).
8. Bake the prepared pizza for about 10-15 minutes

Pasta Frolla

Shortcrust Pastry

SERVINGS: 2   PREPPING TIME: 1 HOUR   COOKING TIME: 45 MIN

INGREDIENTS

300 g of 00 Flour

150 g of Cold Butter, cubed

150 g of Sugar

1 Whole Egg + 1 Yolk

Grated zest of 1 Lemon

A pinch of Salt

DIRECTIONS

1. In the bowl of a stand mixer or on a work surface, pour the flour, sugar, salt, and grated lemon zest.
2. Add the cold cubed butter and work until you obtain a crumbly mixture.
3. Add the egg and the yolk and knead until you get a homogeneous dough.
4. Wrap the dough in cling film and let it rest in the refrigerator for at least 30 minutes before using.

Antipasti

Appetizers

Insalata Russa

Russian Salad

SERVINGS: 2   PREPPING TIME: 15 MIN   COOKING TIME: 30 MIN

INGREDIENTS

1. Boiled potatoes, diced
2. 2 boiled carrots, diced
3. 100g peas, boiled
4. 100g green beans, boiled and chopped
5. 3 boiled eggs, chopped
6. 200g mayonnaise
7. Salt and pepper, to taste
8. Fresh parsley, for garnish

DIRECTIONS

1. In a large bowl, mix together the potatoes, carrots, peas, green beans, and eggs.
2. Add mayonnaise, salt, and pepper, and mix until well combined.
3. Chill in the refrigerator for at least 1 hour before serving.
4. Garnish with fresh parsley before serving.

Sautè di Vongole

Clam Sauté

SERVINGS: 2　　　PREPPING TIME: 10 MIN　　　COOKING TIME: 10 MIN

INGREDIENTS

1 kg fresh Clams, cleaned

2 tbsp Olive Oil

3 Garlic Cloves, minced

1/2 cup White Wine

Fresh Parsley, chopped

Salt and Pepper

Crushed Red Pepper
Flakes (optional)

DIRECTIONS

1. In a large pan, heat olive oil over medium heat. Add garlic and sauté until fragrant.
2. Add the clams and white wine. Cover and simmer until clams open (discard any that do not open).
3. Season with salt, pepper, and red pepper flakes (if using). Garnish with chopped parsley.
4. Serve the clam sauté with crusty bread to soak up the delicious juices.

Torta Rustica con Prosciutto
Rustic Cake with Prosciutto, Potatoes, and Cheese

SERVINGS: 4   PREPPING TIME: 30 MIN   COOKING TIME: 20 MIN

INGREDIENTS

1 roll Puff Pastry

200g Prosciutto Crudo, sliced

2 large Potatoes, sliced

200g Cheese (e.g. Fontina), sliced

1 Egg (for egg wash)

Salt and Pepper

DIRECTIONS

1. Preheat the oven to 200°C (400°F).
2. Roll out the puff pastry and layer with slices of prosciutto, potatoes, and cheese.
3. Season with salt and pepper, fold the pastry to enclose the filling.
4. Brush with beaten egg and bake until golden and puffed.

Polpo e patate

Octopus and Potatoes

SERVINGS: 2   PREPPING TIME: 20 MIN   COOKING TIME: 30 MIN

INGREDIENTS

1 Octopus (about 1kg),
cleaned

500g Potatoes, peeled
and diced

Extra Virgin Olive oil

Fresh Parsley, chopped

Salt and Pepper, to taste

DIRECTIONS

1. Cook the octopus in boiling water until tender,
then let it cool and cut into pieces.
2. Boil the diced potatoes until tender, then drain.
3. In a bowl, mix together the octopus, potatoes,
olive oil, parsley, salt, and pepper.
4. Serve warm or at room temperature.

Polpette di Tonno

Tuna Meatballs

SERVINGS: 6   PREPPING TIME: 20 MIN   COOKING TIME: 20 MIN

INGREDIENTS

400g canned tuna,
drained
1 egg
Breadcrumbs
Parsley, chopped
Salt and pepper, to taste
Olive oil, for frying

DIRECTIONS

1. In a bowl, combine tuna, egg, breadcrumbs, parsley, salt, oil, and pepper.
2. Shape the mixture into small meatballs.
3. In a pan, heat olive oil and fry the meatballs until golden brown on all sides.
4. Serve warm with a side of salad or dipping sauce.

Rustici di sfoglia con verdure

Puff Pastry Rustici with Vegetables

SERVINGS: 4   PREPPING TIME: 20 MIN   COOKING TIME: 20 MIN

INGREDIENTS

1 roll puff pastry
Mixed vegetables (e.g., bell peppers, zucchini), chopped
Olive oil
Salt and pepper
1 egg (for egg wash)

DIRECTIONS

1. Preheat the oven to 200°C (400°F).
2. Sauté the vegetables in olive oil until tender. Season with salt and pepper.
3. Cut the puff pastry into squares and place a spoonful of vegetables in the center.
4. Fold the pastry over the vegetables to form a triangle and seal the edges.
5. Brush with beaten egg and bake until golden brown.

Pizzelle Fritte Napoletane

Neapolitan Fried Pizzelle

SERVINGS: 4   PREPPING TIME: 120 MIN   COOKING TIME: 2 MIN

INGREDIENTS

500g all-purpose flour

250ml warm water

7g active dry yeast

1 tsp sugar

1 tsp salt

Vegetable oil, for frying

Salt, for sprinkling

DIRECTIONS

1. In a bowl, dissolve the yeast and sugar in warm water and let it sit for 10 minutes.
2. Gradually add the flour and salt, mixing until a dough forms.
3. Knead the dough on a floured surface until smooth, then let it rise in a warm place for 1-2 hours.
4. Divide the dough into small balls and roll out into thin discs.
5. Heat the oil in a frying pan and fry the pizzelle until golden brown on both sides.
6. Drain on paper towels and sprinkle with salt while still hot.

Insalata di Polpo

Octopus Salad

SERVINGS: 2   PREPPING TIME: 20 MIN   COOKING TIME:60 MIN

INGREDIENTS

1 Octopus (about 1kg),
cleaned
1 Lemon, juiced
1 Garlic clove, minced
Extra Virgin Olive oil
Fresh Parsley, chopped
Salt and Pepper, to taste

DIRECTIONS

1. Cook the octopus in boiling water until tender, then let it cool and cut into pieces.
2. In a bowl, combine the octopus pieces, lemon juice, garlic, olive oil, parsley, salt, and pepper.
3. Mix well and refrigerate for at least 1 hour before serving.

Torta Rustica con Spinaci e Salsiccia

Rustic Pie with Spinach and Sausage

SERVINGS: 4   PREPPING TIME: 15 MIN   COOKING TIME: 20 MIN

INGREDIENTS

1 Pie crust

300g fresh spinach

200g sausage (crumbled)

200g ricotta cheese

1 egg

Salt and Pepper, to taste

Grated Parmesan cheese

DIRECTIONS

1. Preheat the oven to 375°F (190°C).
2. In a pan, sauté the spinach until wilted, and cook the sausage until browned.
3. In a bowl, mix together the spinach, sausage, ricotta, egg, salt, and pepper.
4. Pour the mixture into the pie crust, and sprinkle with Parmesan cheese.
5. Bake in the preheated oven for about 20 minutes, or until the crust is golden and the filling is set.

Pasta e Risotto

Pasta and Risotto

Pasta alla Norma

Pasta alla Norma

SERVINGS: 4   PREPPING TIME: 15 MIN   COOKING TIME: 20 MIN

INGREDIENTS

400g of pasta (rigatoni or spaghetti)

2 large eggplants

400g of peeled tomatoes

2 cloves of garlic

Ricotta salata, to taste

Fresh basil

Olive oil

Salt

DIRECTIONS

1. Cut the eggplants into cubes and fry in olive oil until golden. Drain them and set aside.
2. In a pan, sauté the garlic in oil, add the tomatoes and salt, and cook for 15-20 minutes.
3. Cook the pasta al dente, drain it, and mix with the tomato sauce.
4. Add the fried eggplants, basil, and grated ricotta salata.
5. Making these slight adjustments would improve the clarity of the instructions.

Risotto con zucchine

Risotto with Zucchini

SERVINGS: 4   PREPPING TIME: 15 MIN   COOKING TIME: 20 MIN

INGREDIENTS

320 g Carnaroli rice

350 g zucchini

80 g white onions

100 g white wine

50 g butter

70 g Parmigiano Reggiano DOP (to be grated)

To taste, fine salt

To taste, black pepper

A drizzle of extra virgin olive oil

5 mint leaves

DIRECTIONS

1. Sauté onions: In a saucepan, heat olive oil, add chopped onions, and sauté until translucent.
2. Toast rice: Add Carnaroli rice to the saucepan, ensuring it's well-coated with oil, and toast until slightly translucent.
3. Deglaze with wine: Pour in white wine, stirring until it has mostly evaporated.
4. Cook risotto: Gradually add warm vegetable broth, one ladle at a time, stirring until the rice is al dente, for about 15-18 minutes.
5. Prepare zucchini: In a separate pan, sauté grated zucchini with olive oil, salt, and pepper until just cooked but still crunchy.
6. Combine zucchini and risotto: Stir the sautéed zucchini into the risotto about 5 minutes before it's done.

Risotto ai funghi

Mushroom Risotto

SERVINGS: 4   PREPPING TIME: 15 MIN   COOKING TIME: 20 MIN

INGREDIENTS

320 g arborio rice

300 g mixed mushrooms (such as porcini, shiitake, and cremini), cleaned and sliced

1 L chicken or vegetable broth

1 small onion, finely chopped

2 garlic cloves, minced

150 ml dry white wine

50 g parmesan cheese, grated

2 tbsp olive oil

30 g butter

Salt, to taste

Freshly ground black pepper, to taste

Fresh parsley, chopped (for garnish)

DIRECTIONS

1. Prepare broth: Warm chicken or vegetable broth in a saucepan over low heat.

2. Sauté mushrooms: In a skillet, heat olive oil and brown the mushrooms for 5-7 minutes, then set aside.

3. Cook onions and garlic: In the same skillet, sauté chopped onions and minced garlic in olive oil and butter until fragrant.

4. Toast rice: Add Arborio rice, stirring until the edges become translucent.

5. Cook risotto: Gradually add warm broth, stirring until the rice is al dente, about 18-20 minutes.

6. Combine and finish: Return the mushrooms to the skillet, stir in the Parmesan and butter, and season with salt and pepper.

7. Serve: Garnish the risotto with chopped parsley and serve hot.

Penne Pomodoro e Basilico

Tomato and Basil Penne

SERVINGS: 4   PREPPING TIME: 15 MIN   COOKING TIME: 20 MIN

INGREDIENTS

400g (14 oz) pasta (such as spaghetti or penne)

2 tablespoons olive oil

1 onion, finely chopped

3 cloves garlic, minced

800g (28 oz) canned whole tomatoes, crushed by hand

A handful of fresh basil leaves, torn

Salt and black pepper, to taste

Sugar, a pinch (optional)

Grated Parmesan cheese, for serving

Extra virgin olive oil, for drizzling

DIRECTIONS

1. Boil pasta in salted water until al dente; drain, reserving some of the pasta water.
2. In a skillet, sauté onions until translucent; then add garlic and cook until aromatic.
3. Add crushed tomatoes to the skillet; simmer until the sauce thickens.
4. Season sauce with salt, pepper, and a pinch of sugar (if using); stir well.
5. Infuse the sauce with torn fresh basil leaves.
6. Toss the cooked pasta in the sauce, adjusting the thickness with reserved pasta water as needed.
7. Serve hot, garnished with grated Parmesan cheese, a drizzle of extra virgin olive oil, and fresh basil.

Risotto piselli e salmone

Pea and salmon risotto

SERVINGS: 2   PREPPING TIME: 15 MIN   COOKING TIME: 20 MIN

INGREDIENTS

200g Arborio rice

200g smoked salmon, chopped

150g fresh or frozen peas

1 small onion, finely chopped

2 cloves garlic, minced

750ml chicken or vegetable broth, kept warm

125ml white wine

30g butter

2 tablespoons olive oil

Salt and black pepper to taste

Freshly grated Parmesan cheese (optional)

Fresh dill or parsley for garnish

DIRECTIONS

1. Chop onions, mince garlic, and dice smoked salmon. Measure Arborio rice and white wine. Warm broth in a separate pot.

2. Sauté Aromatics**: In a skillet, heat olive oil over medium heat. Sauté onions until translucent, then add garlic until fragrant.

3. Toast Rice: Add Arborio rice, stirring continuously until grains are well-coated and edges start to show translucency.

4. Deglaze: Add white wine, stirring until mostly evaporated.

5. Cook Risotto: Gradually add warm broth, stirring constantly. After 10 minutes, add peas. Continue until rice is al dente and creamy, about 18-20 minutes.

6. Add Salmon: Fold in chopped smoked salmon, cooking an additional 2 minutes until heated.

Rigatoni alla Gricia

Rigatoni with Gricia Sauce

SERVINGS: 4   PREPPING TIME: 15 MIN   COOKING TIME: 10 MIN

INGREDIENTS

400g Rigatoni pasta

150g Guanciale (or pancetta), diced

100g Pecorino Romano cheese, grated

Black pepper, freshly ground

Salt

Olive oil (optional)

DIRECTIONS

1. Prep Ingredients: Dice guanciale and grate Pecorino Romano cheese.
2. Cook Guanciale: In a large skillet, cook the guanciale over medium heat until it's crispy, around 7-10 minutes. Remove from heat.
3. Boil Pasta: Cook rigatoni in a large pot of salted boiling water until al dente. Reserve a cup of pasta water and drain the rest.
4. Combine Pasta and Guanciale: Add the drained pasta to skillet with guanciale, tossing to combine.
5. Add Cheese: Remove the skillet from heat. Add Pecorino Romano, stirring quickly, and adding reserved pasta water a bit at a time until creamy.
6. Season: Season generously with freshly ground black pepper.
7. Serve: Serve immediately, possibly with additional cheese or black pepper if desired.

Ragù in Bianco

White Ragù

SERVINGS: 4   PREPPING TIME: 15 MIN   COOKING TIME: 120 MIN

INGREDIENTS

500g Ground meat (mix of beef and pork)

1 Onion, finely chopped

1 Carrot, finely chopped

1 Celery stalk, finely chopped

1 Glass White wine

Olive oil

Salt and pepper

Beef or chicken broth (optional)

Parmesan cheese, for serving

DIRECTIONS

1. Prepare Vegetables: Finely chop onion, carrot, and celery.
2. Sauté Vegetables: Heat olive oil in a pot, and sauté the vegetables until softened.
3. Brown the Meat: Add the ground meat, breaking it up and cooking until browned.
4. Deglaze with Wine: Pour in the white wine, letting it simmer until reduced.
5. Simmer: If using, add a little broth and let the ragù simmer for 1-2 hours. If not, just let it cook for a shorter time, until flavorful.
6. Season: Season with salt and pepper to taste.
7. Serve: Serve over pasta, polenta, or as desired, topped with Parmesan cheese.

Cannelloni

Cannelloni

SERVINGS: 4   PREPPING TIME: 60 MIN   COOKING TIME: 30 MIN

INGREDIENTS

Cannelloni tubes

500g Spinach, cooked
and chopped

250g Ricotta cheese

100g Parmesan cheese,
grated

1 Egg

Nutmeg, to taste

Salt and pepper

Tomato sauce

Béchamel sauce

Mozzarella cheese, for
topping

DIRECTIONS

1. Preheat Oven: Preheat your oven to 180°C
   (350°F).
2. Prepare Filling: Mix spinach, ricotta, half of the
   Parmesan, egg, nutmeg, salt, and pepper in a
   bowl.
3. Fill Cannelloni: Fill the cannelloni tubes with
   the spinach and ricotta mixture.
4. Layer: In a baking dish, spread a layer of tomato
   sauce, place the filled cannelloni on top, then
   cover with béchamel sauce.
5. Top: Sprinkle with mozzarella and the
   remaining Parmesan cheese.
6. Bake: Bake for about 30 minutes, or until
   golden and bubbling.

Penne speck e zucchine

Penne speck and zucchini

SERVINGS: 4   PREPPING TIME: 15 MIN   COOKING TIME: 20 MIN

INGREDIENTS

320g Penne pasta

150g Speck (smoked prosciutto), thinly sliced

2 medium Zucchini, julienned or sliced

1 Onion, finely chopped

2 Garlic cloves, minced

100ml white wine (optional)

Olive oil

Salt and Pepper, to taste

Grated Parmesan cheese, for serving

Fresh basil leaves, for garnish

DIRECTIONS

1. Prepare Ingredients: Slice speck, chop onions, mince garlic, and cut zucchini.

2. Cook Pasta: Boil penne until al dente, drain, reserving some pasta water.

3. Sauté Aromatics: In a skillet, sauté onions and garlic in olive oil until translucent.

4. Add Zucchini: Incorporate zucchini, cooking until tender.

5. Cook Speck: Add speck to the skillet, cooking until slightly crispy.

6. Combine: Deglaze with white wine if using, then toss in the cooked penne, adding reserved pasta water if needed.

7. Season and Serve: Adjust seasoning, garnish with basil and Parmesan, and serve hot.

Pasta alla Puttanesca

Pasta Puttanesca

SERVINGS: 4   PREPPING TIME: 15 MIN   COOKING TIME: 20 MIN

INGREDIENTS

400g of spaghetti

2 cloves of garlic

400g of peeled tomatoes

100g of pitted black olives

2 tablespoons of capers

4 anchovy fillets

Red chili pepper, to taste

Olive oil

Salt

DIRECTIONS

1. In a pan, sauté the garlic, anchovies, and chili pepper in olive oil.
2. Add tomatoes, olives, and capers; cook for 20 minutes.
3. Cook the spaghetti al dente and mix them with the sauce.

Lasagna al Ragù

Lasagna with Ragù

SERVINGS: 4 PREPPING TIME: 30 MIN COOKING TIME: 30 MIN

INGREDIENTS

Lasagna sheets, as
needed
500g of Bolognese sauce
500ml of béchamel sauce
100g of grated Parmesan
cheese

DIRECTIONS

1. In a baking dish, alternate layers of lasagna sheets, Bolognese sauce, béchamel, and Parmesan.
2. Continue until all ingredients are used, finishing with béchamel and Parmesan.
3. Bake in a preheated oven at 180°C for about 30 minutes.

Spaghetti Scampi, arancia e mandorla

Spaghetti with scampi, orange and almond

SERVINGS: 4   PREPPING TIME: 15 MIN   COOKING TIME: 10 MIN

INGREDIENTS

400g Spaghetti
500g Scampi (Shrimp)
1 Orange (zest and juice)
handful of Almonds,
chopped
2 cloves Garlic, minced
Olive Oil
Salt and Pepper, to taste
Fresh Parsley, chopped,
for garnish

DIRECTIONS

1. Cook the spaghetti in a pot of boiling salted water until al dente, then drain.
2. In a large pan, heat olive oil over medium heat and sauté garlic until fragrant.
3. Add scampi to the pan and cook until pink.
4. Stir in the orange zest, orange juice, and chopped almonds.
5. Toss the cooked spaghetti in the pan with the scampi mixture.
6. Season with salt and pepper, garnish with fresh parsley, and serve.

Riso nero zucchine e avocado

Black Rice with Zucchini and Avocado

SERVINGS: 2   PREPPING TIME: 15 MIN   COOKING TIME: 30 MIN

INGREDIENTS

200g Black Rice (Riso
Venere)
2 Zucchinis, sliced
1 Avocado, peeled and
diced
Olive Oil
Salt and Pepper, to taste
Fresh Basil, for garnish

DIRECTIONS

1. Cook the black rice according to the package instructions.
2. In a pan, heat olive oil and sauté zucchini slices until tender.
3. In a bowl, mix the cooked rice, sautéed zucchini, and diced avocado.
4. Season with salt and pepper and garnish with fresh basil before serving.

Rigatoni ripieni con Ragù di salsiccia
Ricotta-Stuffed Rigatoni with Sausage Ragù

SERVINGS: 4   PREPPING TIME: 20 MIN   COOKING TIME: 30 MIN

INGREDIENTS

400g Rigatoni

250g Ricotta Cheese

400g Sausage (crumbled)

800g Tomato Sauce

1 Onion (chopped)

Olive Oil

Salt and Pepper (to taste)

Fresh Basil Leaves (for garnish)

DIRECTIONS

1. Cook the rigatoni in boiling salted water until slightly undercooked, then drain.
2. Fill each rigatoni with ricotta cheese using a pastry bag.
3. In a pan, sauté the onion in olive oil, add the crumbled sausage, and cook until browned.
4. Pour in the tomato sauce, season with salt and pepper, and simmer.
5. Arrange the stuffed rigatoni in a baking dish, cover with the sausage ragù, and bake in a preheated oven until heated through.
6. Garnish with fresh basil leaves and serve.

Risotto alla Zucca

Pumpkin Risotto

SERVINGS: 2/3   PREPPING TIME: 15 MIN   COOKING TIME: 20 MIN

INGREDIENTS

320g (1 1/2 cups)
Carnaroli rice

400g (about 2 cups)
pumpkin, diced

1 onion, finely chopped

1L (4 cups) vegetable
broth

50g (about 4 tbsp) butter

50g (about 1/2 cup) grated
Parmesan cheese

Salt and pepper, to taste

Olive oil

DIRECTIONS

1. In a pan, sauté the diced pumpkin and chopped onion in olive oil until softened.
2. Add the rice and toast it for a few minutes.
3. Gradually add the hot vegetable broth, stirring continuously until the rice is cooked (around 18 minutes).
4. Finish with butter and grated Parmesan cheese, stir well.
5. Adjust the seasoning with salt and pepper, and serve warm.

Spaghetti alla Carbonara

Spaghetti Carbonara

SERVINGS: 4   PREPPING TIME: 15 MIN   COOKING TIME: 15 MIN

INGREDIENTS

400g of spaghetti
150g of guanciale
4 Egg yolks
100g of grated Pecorino
Romano cheese
Black pepper, to taste

DIRECTIONS

1. In a pan, brown the diced guanciale until crispy.
2. Cook the spaghetti in salted water and drain al dente, reserving some cooking water.
3. In a bowl, beat the yolks with Pecorino and pepper.
4. Add the pasta cooking water and continue to whisk the egg yolk with pecorino and pepper.
5. Once you have obtained a cream and the pasta is cooked, turn off the heat and add this cream to the pasta with the heat off.
6. Add the guanciale and serve immediately.

Risotto alla Pescatora

Seafood risotto

SERVINGS: 2/3   PREPPING TIME: 20 MIN   COOKING TIME: 30 MIN

INGREDIENTS

350 g of Carnaroli rice

500 g of mussels

300 g of clams

200 g of squid

200 g of shrimp

1 onion

1 carrot

1 celery stalk

1 clove of garlic

100 ml of white wine

100 g of tomato sauce

Extra virgin olive oil

Salt

Pepper

Parsley

DIRECTIONS

1. Prepare the fish stock. In a large pot, sauté the finely chopped onion, carrot, and celery with a drizzle of extra virgin olive oil. Add the shrimp shells, salt, and pepper and cook for 5 minutes. Pour in the water, bring to a boil, and cook for about 30 minutes. Strain the broth and set it aside.

2. In a large pot, sauté the finely chopped garlic with a drizzle of extra virgin olive oil.

3. Toast the rice. Add the rice to the sauté and toast it for a couple of minutes, stirring continuously.

4. Deglaze the rice with the white wine and let the alcohol completely evaporate.

5. Add the fish stock and the seafood.

6. Add the tomato sauce, chopped parsley, salt, and pepper. Mix well and let the risotto cream for a minute

Pasta alla Boscaiola

Woodman's Pasta

SERVINGS: 4   PREPPING TIME: 15 MIN   COOKING TIME: 15 MIN

INGREDIENTS

400g of pasta (penne or rigatoni)

200g of mixed mushrooms

100g of diced pancetta

200ml of cooking cream

1 onion

Grated Parmigiano Reggiano

Olive oil

Salt and pepper

DIRECTIONS

1. In a pan, sauté the onion and pancetta in oil.
2. Add the mushrooms and cook for 10 minutes.
3. Pour in the cream, cook for another 5 minutes and adjust the seasoning with salt and pepper.
4. Cook the pasta al dente, drain and mix it with the sauce in the pan.
5. Sprinkle with Parmigiano Reggiano and serve.

Pasta e Fagioli

Pasta and Beans

SERVINGS: 2   PREPPING TIME: 15 MIN   COOKING TIME: 30 MIN

INGREDIENTS

200g of mixed pasta

400g of borlotti beans

1 onion

1 carrot

1 celery stalk

1 sprig of rosemary

400g of peeled tomatoes

Vegetable broth

Olive oil

Salt and pepper

DIRECTIONS

1. In a pot, sauté onion, carrot, and celery in oil.
2. Add the beans, tomatoes, and rosemary.
3. Cook, adding broth as necessary.
4. Midway through cooking, add the pasta and cook until al dente.

Rigatoni all'Amatriciana

Rigatoni Amatriciana

SERVINGS: 4   PREPPING TIME: 15 MIN   COOKING TIME: 10 MIN

INGREDIENTS

400g Rigatoni
150g Guanciale, diced
1 can Tomato Passata
1 Red Chili, chopped
100g Pecorino Romano
Cheese, grated
Salt and Pepper

DIRECTIONS

1. In a pan, sauté guanciale until crispy.
2. Add chili and tomato passata, season with salt and pepper, and simmer.
3. Cook rigatoni until al dente, drain and toss with the sauce.
4. Serve with grated Pecorino Romano.

Spaghetti alle Vongole

Spaghetti with clams

SERVINGS: 4   PREPPING TIME: 15 MIN   COOKING TIME: 10 MIN

INGREDIENTS

400g of spaghetti

1kg of clams

2 cloves of garlic

Chili pepper, to taste

Chopped parsley

Olive oil

White Wine

DIRECTIONS

1. In a pan, sauté the garlic and chili pepper in oil, then add the clams and cover.
2. Pour in a glass of white wine.
3. Once the clams have opened, cook the spaghetti until al dente and combine them in the pan.
4. Continue to sauté the spaghetti in the pan, mixing them with the rest of the ingredients. Add the pasta boiling water and continue to stir until a creamy sauce forms (about 3-4 minutes).
5. Sprinkle with parsley and serve immediately.

Spaghetti Olio e Limone

Spaghetti with Oil and Lemon

SERVINGS: 4   PREPPING TIME: 5 MIN   COOKING TIME: 15 MIN

INGREDIENTS

400g Spaghetti

Zest and Juice of 1 Lemon

4 tbsp Extra Virgin Olive Oil

Salt, to taste

Parmesan Cheese, grated, for serving

Fresh Parsley, chopped, for garnish

DIRECTIONS

1. Cook the spaghetti in a large pot of boiling salted water until al dente.
2. In a bowl, mix together the olive oil, lemon zest, and lemon juice.
3. Drain the spaghetti and toss with the lemon and oil mixture.
4. Season with salt, sprinkle with Parmesan cheese and fresh parsley before serving.

Pomodori con Riso

Tomatoes Stuffed with Rice

SERVINGS: 2/3   PREPPING TIME: 15 MIN   COOKING TIME: 90 MIN

INGREDIENTS

6 large tomatoes

1 cup Arborio rice

2 cloves garlic, finely
chopped

A handful of fresh basil,
chopped

Salt and pepper, to taste

Olive oil

2 potatoes (optional),
sliced into thin wedges

1 cup water or vegetable
broth

DIRECTIONS

1. Preheat the oven to 180°C (350°F).
2. Prepare tomatoes by removing tops and scooping out pulp; place them in a baking dish.
3. Mix tomato pulp with rice, garlic, basil, salt, pepper, and olive oil; let it sit for 30 minutes.
4. Stuff tomatoes with the rice mixture, replace the lids, and optionally surround with potato wedges.
5. Add water or broth to the dish, drizzle olive oil, and season.
6. Bake for 1 to 1.25 hours, checking and adding liquid as needed.
7. Ensure the rice is cooked and tomatoes are tender.
8. Let the tomatoes rest briefly after removal from the oven.
9. Serve the tomatoes warm, optionally with the roasted potatoes.

Penne al Salmone

Penne with Salmon

SERVINGS: 4   PREPPING TIME: 15 MIN   COOKING TIME:10 MIN

INGREDIENTS

400g Penne Pasta

200g Smoked Salmon (chopped)

1 cup Heavy Cream

1 tbsp Olive Oil

Salt and Pepper, to taste

Fresh Dill, for garnish

DIRECTIONS

1. Cook the penne pasta according to package instructions.
2. In a pan, heat olive oil and add chopped salmon.
3. Pour in heavy cream and simmer until the sauce has thickened.
4. Toss the cooked pasta in the sauce and season with salt and pepper.
5. Garnish with fresh dill before serving.

Crepes Salate Ripieni di Funghi

Savory Crepes Stuffed with Mushrooms

SERVINGS: 2   PREPPING TIME: 40 MIN   COOKING TIME: 20 MIN

INGREDIENTS

For the Crepes:

1 cup All-Purpose Flour

1 ½ cups Milk

2 Eggs

Pinch of Salt

Butter (for cooking)

For the Filling:

400g Mixed Mushrooms (sliced)

1 Onion (finely chopped)

2 Garlic Cloves (minced)

Olive Oil

Salt and Pepper (to taste)

Fresh Parsley (chopped, for garnish)

DIRECTIONS

1. In a bowl, whisk together the flour, milk, eggs, and salt until smooth.
2. In a skillet, melt a little butter and pour in some batter to form a crepe. Cook both sides until golden. Repeat with the remaining batter.
3. Prepare the Filling:
4. In the same skillet, sauté the onion and garlic in olive oil until soft.
5. Add the mushrooms and cook until tender. Season with salt and pepper.
6. Assemble and Serve:
7. Fill each crepe with the mushroom mixture, fold, and garnish with fresh parsley. Serve warm.

Ragù alla Bolognese

Bolognese sauce

SERVINGS: 4   PREPPING TIME: 30 MIN   COOKING TIME: 180 MIN

INGREDIENTS

400g Minced Beef

200g Minced Pork

1 Onion (finely chopped)

1 Carrot (finely chopped)

1 Celery Stick (finely chopped)

150ml Red Wine

800g Crushed Tomatoes

2 tbsp Olive Oil

Salt and Pepper (to taste)

Freshly Grated Parmesan Cheese (for serving)

DIRECTIONS

1. In a large pot, heat olive oil and sauté the onion, carrot, and celery until soft.
2. Add the minced beef and pork, cooking until browned.
3. Pour in the red wine and let it reduce.
4. Add the crushed tomatoes, season with salt and pepper, and simmer for at least 2 to 4 hours.
5. Serve the Bolognese sauce over pasta and garnish with Parmesan cheese.

Rigatoni Cacio e Pepe

Rigatoni with Cheese and Pepper

SERVINGS: 4 PREPPING TIME: 10 MIN COOKING TIME: 10 MIN

INGREDIENTS

400g Rigatoni
200g Pecorino Romano
Cheese, grated
Black Pepper, freshly
ground, to taste
Salt

DIRECTIONS

1. Cook the rigatoni in salted boiling water until al dente.
2. Reserve some of the pasta cooking water and drain the rest.
3. In a bowl, mix grated Pecorino Romano cheese with some of the reserved pasta cooking water until it becomes creamy.
4. Toss the cooked rigatoni in the cheese mixture, add plenty of freshly ground black pepper, mix well, and serve immediately.

Secondi Piatti

Main Courses

Saltimbocca alla romana

Roman-Style Saltimbocca

SERVINGS: 2   PREPPING TIME: 15 MIN   COOKING TIME: 15 MIN

INGREDIENTS

4 veal slices

4 slices of prosciutto

4 sage leaves

Flour, for dusting

White wine

Butter

Salt and pepper, to taste

Olive oil

DIRECTIONS

1. Place a sage leaf on each veal slice and cover it with a slice of prosciutto, securing them together with a toothpick.
2. Lightly dust each veal slice with flour.
3. In a pan, heat a mixture of olive oil and butter.
4. Add the veal slices with the prosciutto side down and cook until they are browned.
5. Flip the veal slices and cook the other side.
6. Add a splash of white wine, let it evaporate, and season the dish with salt and pepper.
7. Serve the veal saltimbocca hot.

Pollo al limone

Lemon Chicken

SERVINGS: 2   PREPPING TIME: 15 MIN   COOKING TIME: 40 MIN

INGREDIENTS

300 g Chicken pieces
Juice of 2 lemons
Olive Oil
Salt and Pepper (to taste)
Fresh herbs (such as
rosemary or thyme,
optional)

DIRECTIONS

1. Marinate the chicken pieces in lemon juice, olive oil, salt, pepper, and optionally, herbs.
2. Preheat the oven to 400°F (200°C).
3. Arrange the marinated chicken pieces in a baking dish.
4. Bake until the chicken is golden brown and cooked through, basting occasionally with the marinade to keep it moist.
5. Serve the lemon chicken hot, and you can drizzle the cooking juices over it for added flavor.

Melanzane alla parmigiana

Eggplant Parmesan

SERVINGS: 2   PREPPING TIME: 45 MIN   COOKING TIME: 30 MIN

INGREDIENTS

2 large Eggplants
2 cups Tomato Sauce
2 cups Mozzarella Cheese
(shredded)
1 cup Parmesan Cheese
(grated)
Fresh Basil Leaves
Salt and Olive Oil (for
frying)

DIRECTIONS

1. Slice the eggplants and salt them to draw out excess moisture. Rinse and pat dry.
2. Fry the eggplant slices in olive oil until golden, then drain them on paper towels.
3. In a baking dish, layer the fried eggplant slices with tomato sauce, mozzarella, Parmesan, and basil.
4. Bake in a preheated oven at 375°F (190°C) until bubbly and golden.
5. Serve hot.

Polpettone Spinaci e Formaggio

Spinach and Cheese Meatloaf

SERVINGS: 4   PREPPING TIME: 30 MIN   COOKING TIME: 50 MIN

INGREDIENTS

800g of ground meat (beef or mixed)

200g of fresh spinach

150g of cheese (mozzarella, fontina, or provola), diced

1 egg

50g of breadcrumbs

50ml of milk

1 small onion, finely chopped

Salt and pepper, to taste

Nutmeg, to taste

Olive oil, as needed

Tomato sauce, as needed (optional)

DIRECTIONS

1. In a large pan, sauté the onion in olive oil until it becomes transparent.
2. Add the spinach and cook until wilted.
3. In a large bowl, mix the ground meat, egg, breadcrumbs, milk, salt, pepper, and nutmeg until you get a homogeneous mixture.
4. Spread the mixture on a sheet of parchment paper, forming a rectangle about 1 cm thick.
5. Filling: Distribute the cooked spinach and diced cheese on the mixture, leaving a free edge all around.
6. Roll the meatloaf using the parchment paper and seal the edges well to prevent filling from leaking during cooking.
7. Preheat the oven to 180°C (350°F).
8. Bake for about 45-50 minutes or until the meatloaf is cooked and golden.

Pollo alla Romana

Roman-Style Chicken

SERVINGS: 2   PREPPING TIME: 15 MIN   COOKING TIME: 45 MIN

INGREDIENTS

500 g Chicken pieces
1 Onion (chopped)
1 Red Bell Pepper (sliced)
1 cup Tomato Sauce
White Wine (optional)
Olive Oil
Salt and Pepper (to taste)
Fresh herbs (such as rosemary or sage, optional)

DIRECTIONS

1. In a large skillet, heat olive oil and brown the chicken pieces on all sides.
2. Add chopped onion and bell pepper, sautéing until softened.
3. Pour in the tomato sauce and white wine if using. Season with salt, pepper, and herbs if using.
4. Cover and simmer until the chicken is cooked through and the sauce has thickened.
5. Serve the Roman-style chicken hot with its sauce.

Polpette al Sugo

Meathalls in Tomato Sauce

SERVINGS: 4   PREPPING TIME: 15 MIN   COOKING TIME: 30 MIN

INGREDIENTS

500g of ground meat
(mixed beef and pork)

1 egg

50g of grated Parmesan
cheese

Breadcrumbs, as needed

Salt and pepper

1L of tomato passata

1 onion

Olive oil

Fresh basil

DIRECTIONS

1. In a bowl, mix meat, egg, Parmesan, breadcrumbs, salt, and pepper.
2. Form the mixture into meatballs and set them aside.
3. In a pan, sauté the chopped onion in olive oil, add the tomato passata, salt, and basil.
4. Add the meatballs to the sauce and simmer for about 30 minutes.

Arrosto di Manzo

Stuffed Roast Beef Roll

SERVINGS: 2/4   PREPPING TIME: 15 MIN   COOKING TIME: 90 MIN

INGREDIENTS

1 large Beef Slice (for rolling)
100g Bread Crumbs
50g Grated Parmesan Cheese
2 Garlic Cloves (minced)
Fresh Parsley (chopped)
Salt and Pepper (to taste)
Olive Oil
Kitchen String (for tying)

DIRECTIONS

1. Mix bread crumbs, Parmesan cheese, garlic, parsley, salt, and pepper to make the stuffing.
2. Lay the beef slice flat, spread the stuffing over it, and roll it up tightly.
3. Tie the beef roll securely with kitchen string.
4. In a pan, sear the beef roll in olive oil until browned on all sides.
5. Transfer to a preheated oven and roast until cooked to your liking.
6. Let it rest before slicing. Serve the stuffed roast beef roll warm.

Scaloppine al limone

Lemon Scaloppine

SERVINGS: 2   PREPPING TIME: 15 MIN   COOKING TIME:15 MIN

INGREDIENTS

4 veal slices

Flour, for dusting

Juice of 1 lemon

Chicken broth

Butter

Olive oil

Salt and pepper, to taste

Fresh parsley, chopped
(for garnish)

DIRECTIONS

1. Dust the veal slices with flour, shaking off any excess.
2. In a skillet, heat olive oil and butter over medium heat.
3. Add the veal slices and cook until browned on both sides.
4. Add the lemon juice and a bit of chicken broth, and let it simmer for a few minutes.
5. Season with salt and pepper.
6. Garnish with chopped parsley and serve warm.

Cotoletta alla Milanese

Milanese Cutlet

SERVINGS: 2   PREPPING TIME: 15 MIN   COOKING TIME: 5 MIN

INGREDIENTS

4 Veal Cutlets (bone-in)

2 Eggs (beaten)

1 cup Bread Crumbs

Salt (to taste)

Olive Oil or Butter (for frying)

Lemon Wedges (for serving)

DIRECTIONS

1. Season the veal cutlets with salt and dip each one first in the beaten eggs, then coat with bread crumbs.
2. In a skillet, heat the olive oil or butter and fry the cutlets until golden brown on both sides.
3. Serve the cutlets hot, garnished with lemon wedges.

Calamari Ripieni

Stuffed Squid

SERVINGS: 2   PREPPING TIME: 15 MIN   COOKING TIME: 30 MIN

INGREDIENTS

6 Large Squids (cleaned, tentacles reserved)

2 cups Fresh Bread Crumbs

1 Garlic Clove (minced)

2 tbsp Parsley (chopped)

1/4 cup Grated Parmesan Cheese

Olive Oil

Salt and Pepper (to taste)

Marinara Sauce (for serving)

DIRECTIONS

1. Prepare the Filling:
2. Chop the reserved squid tentacles.
3. In a bowl, mix together the chopped tentacles, bread crumbs, garlic, parsley, Parmesan, olive oil, salt, and pepper.
4. Stuff the Squids:
5. Stuff each squid with the filling and secure the opening with toothpicks.
6. Cook the Stuffed Squids:
7. In a skillet, sear the stuffed squids in olive oil until browned on all sides.
8. Add some marinara sauce to the skillet, cover, and simmer until the squids are tender.
9. Serve the stuffed squids hot with additional marinara sauce.

Pesce Spada Gratinato al Forno

Baked Swordfish Gratin

SERVINGS: 4   PREPPING TIME: 15 MIN   COOKING TIME: 25 MIN

INGREDIENTS

4 Swordfish Steaks
Breadcrumbs
Grated Parmesan Cheese
Olive oil
Salt and Pepper, to taste
Lemon Wedges, for
serving

DIRECTIONS

1. Preheat the oven to 180°C (350°F).
2. Place the swordfish steaks in a baking dish.
3. In a bowl, mix breadcrumbs and Parmesan. Sprinkle the mixture over the swordfish steaks.
4. Drizzle with olive oil, season with salt and pepper, and bake until golden and cooked through.
5. Serve with lemon wedges.

Platessa Panata

Breaded Plaice

SERVINGS: 2   PREPPING TIME: 15 MIN   COOKING TIME: 10 MIN

INGREDIENTS

4 Plaice Fillets

1 cup Breadcrumbs

2 Eggs (beaten)

Salt and Pepper (to taste)

Olive Oil (for frying)

Lemon Wedges (for serving)

DIRECTIONS

1. Season the plaice fillets with salt and pepper.
2. Dip each fillet in beaten eggs, then coat with breadcrumbs.
3. In a skillet, heat olive oil over medium heat and fry the fillets until golden brown on both sides.
4. Serve hot with lemon wedges.

Omelette

Omelette

SERVINGS: 2   PREPPING TIME: 15 MIN   COOKING TIME: 10 MIN

INGREDIENTS

3 Eggs

Salt and Pepper (to taste)

2 tbsp Milk or Cream

Butter or Olive Oil (for cooking)

Optional Fillings: Cheese, Ham, Vegetables, Herbs

DIRECTIONS

1. In a bowl, whisk together eggs, milk/cream, salt, and pepper.
2. In a skillet, melt butter or heat olive oil over medium heat.
3. Pour in the egg mixture and cook until almost set, adding fillings if desired.
4. Fold the omelette in half and serve warm.

Salmone in Padella

Pan-Seared Salmon

SERVINGS: 4   PREPPING TIME: 10 MIN   COOKING TIME: 10 MIN

INGREDIENTS

4 Salmon Fillets
Salt and Pepper (to taste)
Olive Oil
Lemon Juice
Fresh Herbs (e.g. dill, parsley)

DIRECTIONS

1. Season the salmon fillets with salt, pepper, and lemon juice.
2. In a skillet, heat olive oil over medium-high heat.
3. Sear the salmon fillets skin-side down first, then flip and cook until desired doneness.
4. Serve hot, garnished with fresh herbs.

Frittata di Cipolle

Onion Frittata

SERVINGS: 2/4   **PREPPING TIME: 15 MIN**   **COOKING TIME: 10 MIN**

INGREDIENTS

6 Eggs
2 large Onions (sliced)
Salt and Pepper (to taste)
Olive Oil
Grated Parmesan Cheese
(optional)

DIRECTIONS

1. In a skillet, sauté the sliced onions in olive oil until caramelized.
2. In a bowl, whisk together eggs, salt, pepper, and cheese if using.
3. Pour the egg mixture over the onions and cook until set, flipping once.
4. Serve the frittata warm or at room temperature.

Pesce Spada al Forno

Baked Swordfish

SERVINGS: 4　　　PREPPING TIME: 15 MIN　　　COOKING TIME: 30 MIN

INGREDIENTS

4 Swordfish Steaks

Salt and Pepper, to taste

Olive Oil

1 Lemon (sliced)

Fresh Herbs (such as parsley or thyme)

Cherry Tomatoes (optional)

DIRECTIONS

1. Preheat the oven to 400°F (200°C).
2. Season the swordfish steaks with salt and pepper.
3. Place the steaks in a baking dish, drizzle with olive oil, and top with lemon slices and fresh herbs.
4. If using, add cherry tomatoes around the fish.
5. Bake in the preheated oven for about 15-20 minutes, or until the fish is cooked through.

Bocconcini di Tacchino con Verdure

Turkey Bites with Vegetables in Pan

SERVINGS: 2   PREPPING TIME: 15 MIN   COOKING TIME: 45 MIN

INGREDIENTS

500g Turkey Breast (cut
into bite-sized pieces)
Mixed Vegetables (such
as bell peppers, zucchini,
peppers and eggplatns
cherry tomatoes)
Olive Oil
Salt and Pepper, to taste
Fresh Herbs (such as
rosemary or thyme)

DIRECTIONS

1. In a large pan, heat olive oil over medium heat.
2. Add the turkey bites and cook until browned on all sides.
3. Add the mixed vegetables, salt, pepper, and fresh herbs.
4. Sauté everything together until the vegetables are tender and the turkey is cooked through.

Brasato al Barolo

Braised in Barolo

SERVINGS: 4　　　PREPPING TIME: 30 MIN　　　COOKING TIME: 4 HOURS

INGREDIENTS

1.5 kg Beef Chuck or
Brisket

1 bottle Barolo wine

2 Onions, chopped

2 Carrots, chopped

2 Celery Stalks, chopped

2 Garlic Cloves

4-5 Juniper Berries

1 sprig Rosemary

Salt and Pepper, to taste

Olive oil

Beef Stock (optional)

DIRECTIONS

1. Marinate the beef in Barolo wine with onions, carrots, celery, garlic, juniper berries, and rosemary overnight.
2. Preheat oven to 150°C (300°F). Remove the beef from the marinade and pat dry. In a large ovenproof pan, heat olive oil and brown the beef on all sides.
3. Add the marinade and vegetables to the pan. Season with salt and pepper. Bring to a boil, cover, and transfer to the oven.
4. Cook for 3-4 hours, adding beef stock if necessary, until the beef is tender.
5. Slice the beef and serve with the cooking sauce.

Spiedini di Pesce con Verdure

Fish Skewers with Vegetables

SERVINGS: 2   PREPPING TIME: 15 MIN   COOKING TIME: 10 MIN

INGREDIENTS

500g Mixed Fish (such as
shrimp, scallops, and
firm white fish), cut into
bite-sized pieces
Mixed Vegetables (such
as bell peppers, zucchini,
cherry tomatoes)
Olive Oil
Salt and Pepper, to taste
Lemon Wedges, for
serving

DIRECTIONS

1. Preheat the grill or broiler.
2. Thread the fish pieces and vegetables onto skewers, alternating between the two.
3. Brush the skewers with olive oil and season with salt and pepper.
4. Grill or broil the skewers for about 6-8 minutes, turning occasionally, until the fish is cooked and the vegetables are tender.
5. Serve the skewers hot with lemon wedges on the side.

Scaloppine al Marsala

Marsala Veal Scaloppini

SERVINGS: 2   PREPPING TIME: 15 MIN   COOKING TIME: 15 MIN

INGREDIENTS

4 Veal or Turkey Cutlets
Salt and Pepper, to taste
Flour, for dredging
2 tbsp Olive Oil
1 cup Marsala Wine
Fresh Parsley, chopped

DIRECTIONS

1. Season the cutlets with salt and pepper, then dredge in flour.
2. In a pan, heat olive oil and cook the cutlets until browned on both sides.
3. Add Marsala wine and simmer until the wine has reduced and the cutlets are cooked through.
4. Garnish with fresh parsley and serve.

Seppie e Piselli

Cuttlefish and Peas

SERVINGS: 2   PREPPING TIME: 20 MIN   COOKING TIME: 40 MIN

INGREDIENTS

4 Cuttlefish, cleaned and
sliced
300g Fresh or Frozen
Peas
1 Onion, chopped
Olive oil
Salt and Pepper, to taste

DIRECTIONS

1. In a pan, heat olive oil and sauté onion until translucent.
2. Add the cuttlefish and cook for a few minutes.
3. Add peas, season with salt and pepper, cover, and cook until both cuttlefish and peas are tender.
4. Serve warm with crusty bread.

Moscardini al Sugo

Baby Octopus in Tomato Sauce

SERVINGS: 4   PREPPING TIME: 10 MIN   COOKING TIME: 40 MIN

INGREDIENTS

500g Baby Octopus,
cleaned

400g Tomato Sauce

1 Onion, chopped

Olive oil

Salt and Pepper, to taste

Fresh Parsley, chopped

DIRECTIONS

1. In a pan, heat olive oil and sauté onion until translucent.
2. Add the baby octopus and cook for a few minutes.
3. Pour in the tomato sauce, season with salt and pepper, and simmer until the octopus is tender.
4. Garnish with fresh parsley and serve warm.

Pollo al forno con le patate

Baked Chicken and Potatoes

SERVINGS: 2   PREPPING TIME: 15 MIN   COOKING TIME: 50 MIN

INGREDIENTS

4 Chicken Thighs or
Drumsticks
4 Large Potatoes, peeled
and cut into wedges
Olive oil
Salt and Pepper, to taste
Rosemary, fresh or dried
4 Garlic Cloves, minced

DIRECTIONS

1. Preheat the oven to 200°C (400°F).
2. Arrange the chicken and potato wedges in a baking dish.
3. Drizzle with olive oil, season with salt, pepper, rosemary, and garlic.
4. Bake for about 50 minutes or until the chicken is cooked through and potatoes are golden brown.

Burger di Piselli

Pea Burgers

SERVINGS: 4   PREPPING TIME: 20 MIN   COOKING TIME: 10 MIN

INGREDIENTS

400g Frozen Peas,
thawed

1 Egg

50g Breadcrumbs

Salt and Pepper, to taste

Olive oil, for frying

Burger Buns, for serving

Lettuce, Tomato Slices,
and other preferred
toppings

DIRECTIONS

1. In a food processor, blend peas until smooth. Transfer to a bowl and mix with egg, breadcrumbs, salt, and pepper.
2. Shape the mixture into burger patties and fry in olive oil until golden brown on both sides.
3. Assemble the burgers with buns, pea patties, lettuce, tomato slices, and your favorite toppings. Serve immediately.

Pollo al Curry

Chicken Curry

SERVINGS: 2   PREPPING TIME: 15 MIN   COOKING TIME: 30 MIN

INGREDIENTS

500g Chicken breast, diced

1 Onion, finely chopped

2 tbsp Curry powder

400ml Coconut milk

Olive oil

Salt and Pepper, to taste

Fresh Coriander, for garnish

DIRECTIONS

1. In a large pan, heat olive oil and sauté the onion until translucent.
2. Add the chicken pieces and brown on all sides.
3. Sprinkle curry powder over the chicken and stir well.
4. Pour in the coconut milk and simmer for about 20 minutes, until the chicken is cooked through.
5. Season with salt and pepper and garnish with fresh coriander before serving.

Spezzatino con piselli

Stew with Peas

SERVINGS: 2   PREPPING TIME: 15 MIN   COOKING TIME: 90 MIN

INGREDIENTS

500g Beef, cut into cubes

300g Fresh or Frozen Peas

1 Onion, finely chopped

2 Carrots, chopped

2 Celery Stalks, chopped

150ml Tomato Sauce

Olive oil

Salt and Pepper, to taste

Fresh Parsley, chopped (optional, for garnish)

DIRECTIONS

1. In a large pot, heat olive oil and sauté the onion, carrots, and celery until softened.
2. Add the beef cubes and brown on all sides.
3. Stir in the tomato sauce and cook for a few minutes.
4. Add the peas, season with salt and pepper, and simmer until the beef is tender and the peas are cooked, about 30-40 minutes.
5. Garnish with fresh parsley if desired and serve warm.

Carne alla Pizzaiola

Pizzaiola Meat

SERVINGS: 2   PREPPING TIME: 15 MIN   COOKING TIME: 15 MIN

INGREDIENTS

4 Beef Steaks
1 can Crushed Tomatoes
2 Garlic Cloves, minced
Olive Oil
Salt and Pepper, to taste
Fresh Basil or Oregano

DIRECTIONS

1. In a skillet, heat olive oil and sauté garlic until fragrant.
2. Add the steaks and brown on both sides.
3. Pour in the crushed tomatoes, season with salt, pepper, and herbs.
4. Simmer until the meat is tender and the sauce has thickened.

Gamberetti in Padella

Pan-Seared Shrimp

SERVINGS: 2   PREPPING TIME: 15 MIN   COOKING TIME:10 MIN

INGREDIENTS

500g Shrimp (peeled and deveined)

2 tbsp Olive Oil

2 Garlic Cloves (minced)

Salt and Pepper, to taste

Fresh Lemon Juice

Fresh Parsley, chopped

DIRECTIONS

1. In a pan, heat olive oil and sauté garlic until fragrant.
2. Add shrimp, season with salt and pepper, and cook until pink and opaque.
3. Finish with a squeeze of fresh lemon juice and garnish with chopped parsley.

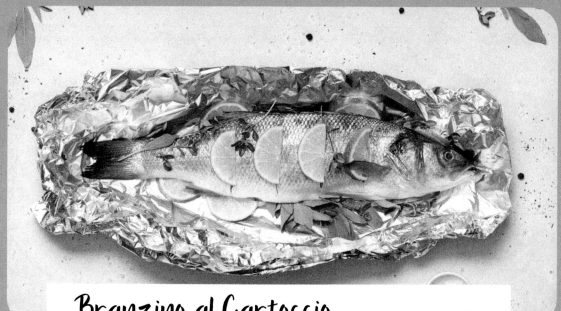

Branzino al Cartoccio

Sea Bass in Parchment

SERVINGS: 2   PREPPING TIME: 15 MIN   COOKING TIME: 20 MIN

INGREDIENTS

2 Sea Bass Fillets

Salt and Pepper, to taste

Olive Oil

Lemon Slices

Fresh Herbs (such as thyme or parsley)

Cherry Tomatoes

DIRECTIONS

1. Preheat the oven to 400°F (200°C).
2. Season the sea bass fillets with salt and pepper and place each on a piece of parchment paper.
3. Drizzle with olive oil and top with lemon slices, fresh herbs, and cherry tomatoes.
4. Fold the parchment paper to create a sealed packet.
5. Bake in the preheated oven for 15-20 minutes, or until the fish is cooked through.

Frittata di Patate

Potato Frittata

SERVINGS: 2   PREPPING TIME: 15 MIN   COOKING TIME: 15 MIN

INGREDIENTS

4-5 medium-sized
Potatoes, peeled and
sliced
6 Eggs
Salt and Pepper, to taste
1/4 cup Grated Parmesan
Cheese
2 tbsp Olive Oil
Fresh Parsley, chopped
(optional)

DIRECTIONS

1. In a skillet, heat olive oil and add the sliced potatoes.
2. Cook until the potatoes are tender and golden brown.
3. In a bowl, whisk together eggs, salt, pepper, and Parmesan cheese.
4. Pour the egg mixture over the potatoes and let it set on the bottom.
5. Flip the frittata and cook until the other side is golden brown.
6. Garnish with fresh parsley, if using, and serve warm.

Gamberoni al Forno

Baked Prawns

SERVINGS: 2   PREPPING TIME: 15 MIN   COOKING TIME: 10 MIN

INGREDIENTS

8 large Prawns, deveined
2 tbsp Olive Oil
Salt and Pepper, to taste
2 Garlic Cloves, minced
Lemon Wedges, for
serving
Fresh Parsley, chopped,
for garnish

DIRECTIONS

1. Preheat the oven to 400°F (200°C).
2. Arrange the prawns in a baking dish and drizzle with olive oil.
3. Season with salt, pepper, and minced garlic.
4. Bake in the preheated oven for 12-15 minutes, or until the prawns are opaque.
5. Serve with lemon wedges and garnish with chopped parsley.

Gamberi in Gabbia

Caged Shrimp

SERVINGS: 4   PREPPING TIME: 20 MIN   COOKING TIME: 10 MIN

INGREDIENTS

12 large Shrimp, peeled
and deveined

1 cup All-Purpose Flour

2 Eggs, beaten

1 cup Breadcrumbs

Salt and Pepper

Oil for frying

Lemon Wedges for
serving

DIRECTIONS

1. Season the shrimp with salt and pepper.
2. Dredge each shrimp in flour, then dip in beaten eggs, and finally coat with breadcrumbs.
3. Heat oil in a deep fryer or large pan over medium-high heat.
4. Fry the shrimp until golden brown and crispy.
5. Drain on paper towels and serve hot with lemon wedges.

Orata in Crosta di Patate

Bream in Potato Crust

SERVINGS: 2   PREPPING TIME: 20 MIN   COOKING TIME: 40 MIN

INGREDIENTS

1 Bream (Orata), cleaned
and gutted
3 Large Potatoes, sliced
Olive Oil
Salt and Pepper
Fresh Herbs (e.g.
rosemary, thyme)

DIRECTIONS

1. Preheat the oven to 180°C (350°F).
2. Season the bream inside and out with salt,
   pepper, and herbs.
3. Arrange the potato slices overlapping on a
   baking tray, place the fish on top.
4. Drizzle with olive oil and bake until potatoes are
   golden and fish is cooked through.

Pesce spada alla siciliana

Sicilian-Style Swordfish

SERVINGS: 4   PREPPING TIME: 15 MIN   COOKING TIME: 30 MIN

INGREDIENTS

4 Swordfish Steaks

Salt and Pepper, to taste

2 tbsp Olive Oil

1 Onion, sliced

1 cup Cherry Tomatoes, halved

1/2 cup Black Olives, pitted and sliced

2 tbsp Capers

Fresh Parsley, chopped

DIRECTIONS

1. Season the swordfish steaks with salt and pepper.
2. In a skillet, heat olive oil and sear the swordfish on both sides until golden.
3. Remove the swordfish and sauté the onion until translucent.
4. Add cherry tomatoes, olives, capers, and cook for a few minutes.
5. Return the swordfish to the skillet and simmer with the sauce until cooked through.
6. Garnish with fresh parsley and serve.

Abbacchio Scottadito

Grilled Lamb Chops

SERVINGS: 4   PREPPING TIME: 15 MIN   COOKING TIME: 5 MIN

INGREDIENTS

8 Lamb Chops
2 Garlic Cloves, minced
2 tbsp Olive Oil
2 tbsp Fresh Rosemary, chopped
Salt and Pepper
Lemon Wedges for serving

DIRECTIONS

1. In a bowl, mix together olive oil, garlic, rosemary, salt, and pepper.
2. Marinate the lamb chops in the mixture for at least 30 minutes.
3. Grill the lamb chops until golden and cooked to your liking.
4. Serve hot with lemon wedges.

Parmigiana Bianca di Zucchine

White Zucchini Parmesan

SERVINGS: 4   PREPPING TIME: 30 MIN   COOKING TIME: 30 MIN

INGREDIENTS

4 Zucchinis, sliced
200g Mozzarella Cheese,
sliced
Grated Parmesan Cheese
Salt and Pepper, to taste
Olive oil
Fresh Basil Leaves

DIRECTIONS

1. Preheat the oven to 200°C (400°F).
2. In a baking dish, layer zucchini slices, mozzarella, Parmesan, salt, pepper, and a drizzle of olive oil. Repeat the layers until all ingredients are used.
3. Bake until golden brown and bubbly.
4. Garnish with fresh basil leaves and serve warm.

Sformato di Patate e Formaggio

Potato and Cheese Flan

SERVINGS: 2   PREPPING TIME: 30 MIN   COOKING TIME: 45 MIN

INGREDIENTS

4 Large Potatoes, peeled and diced

100g Grated Cheese (e.g. Parmesan)

2 Eggs

Salt and Pepper

Butter and Breadcrumbs (for the mold)

DIRECTIONS

1. Preheat the oven to 180°C (350°F).
2. Boil the potatoes until tender, drain and mash.
3. Mix mashed potatoes with eggs, cheese, salt, and pepper.
4. Grease a baking mold with butter, coat with breadcrumbs, pour in the mixture.
5. Bake until golden and set.

Alette di Pollo in Padella

Pan-fried Chicken Wings

SERVINGS: 2   PREPPING TIME: 10 MIN   COOKING TIME: 25 MIN

INGREDIENTS

500g Chicken Wings

2 tbsp Olive Oil

2 Garlic Cloves, minced

Salt and Pepper

1 tbsp Fresh Herbs (e.g. parsley, thyme)

DIRECTIONS

1. Season the chicken wings with salt and pepper.
2. In a pan, heat olive oil and sauté garlic until fragrant.
3. Add the chicken wings and fry until golden and cooked through.
4. Sprinkle with fresh herbs before serving.

Uova all'Occhio di Bue

Sunny Side Up Eggs

SERVINGS: 2   PREPPING TIME: 3 MIN   COOKING TIME: 5 MIN

INGREDIENTS

4 Eggs
Salt and Pepper, to taste
2 tbsp Butter or Olive Oil
Fresh Herbs, for garnish
(optional)

DIRECTIONS

1. In a skillet, heat butter or olive oil over medium heat.
2. Crack the eggs into the skillet, being careful not to break the yolks.
3. Season with salt and pepper.
4. Cook until the whites are set but the yolks remain runny.
5. Garnish with fresh herbs, if using, and serve immediately.

Faraona Ripiena

Stuffed Guinea Fowl

SERVINGS: 2   PREPPING TIME: 30 MIN   COOKING TIME: 90 MIN

INGREDIENTS

1 Guinea Fowl, about 1.5 kg
Salt and Pepper, to taste
100g Ground Meat (Pork or Beef)
50g Bread Crumbs
1 Egg
Fresh Parsley, chopped
2 Garlic Cloves, minced
100ml White Wine
2 tbsp Olive Oil

DIRECTIONS

1. Preheat your oven to 180°C (350°F).
2. Season the guinea fowl with salt and pepper inside and out.
3. In a bowl, mix together the ground meat, bread crumbs, egg, parsley, and garlic to make the stuffing.
4. Stuff the guinea fowl with this mixture.
5. In an ovenproof dish, heat the olive oil and brown the guinea fowl on all sides.
6. Add white wine and let it evaporate.
7. Transfer to the oven and roast for about 1 hour, basting occasionally.

Filetti di Branzino Ripieni con pinoli

Stuffed Sea Bass Fillets with Raisins

SERVINGS: 2   PREPPING TIME: 15 MIN   COOKING TIME: 30 MIN

INGREDIENTS

4 Sea Bass Fillets

Salt and Pepper, to taste

50g Raisins

50g Pine Nuts

Fresh Parsley, chopped

Olive Oil

Lemon Wedges, for
serving

DIRECTIONS

1. Preheat your oven to 180°C (350°F).
2. Season the sea bass fillets with salt and pepper.
3. In a bowl, mix together the raisins, pine nuts, and parsley.
4. Stuff each fillet with this mixture and secure with toothpicks if necessary.
5. Drizzle with olive oil and bake in the preheated oven for 15-20 minutes.
6. Serve with lemon wedges.

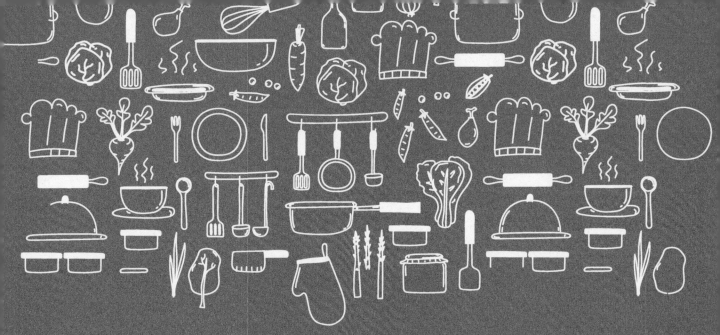

Pizza

Pizza

Pizza Margherita

Margherita Pizza

SERVINGS: 1   PREPPING TIME: 15 MIN   COOKING TIME: 12 MIN

INGREDIENTS

1 Pizza Dough
200g Tomato Sauce
100g Mozzarella Cheese,
shredded
A handful of fresh basil
leaves
2 tablespoons olive oil
Salt, to taste

DIRECTIONS

1. Top the Pizza: a. Spread a layer of tomato sauce over the dough, leaving a small border around the edges. b. Scatter the mozzarella cheese evenly over the sauce. c. Drizzle a bit of olive oil over the top and sprinkle with a pinch of salt.
2. Bake the Pizza: a. If using a pizza stone, slide the pizza onto the stone in the preheated oven. If using a baking sheet, simply place the sheet in the oven. b. Bake for about 8-12 minutes, or until the crust is golden and the cheese is melted and slightly bubbly.
3. Final Touches: a. Immediately top the hot pizza with fresh basil leaves.
4. Drizzle a bit more olive oil over the top if desired.
5. Slice and serve immediately.

Pizza Napoli

Napoli Pizza

SERVINGS: 1   PREPPING TIME: 15 MIN   COOKING TIME: 12 MIN

INGREDIENTS

1 Pizza Dough

200g Tomato Sauce

100g Mozzarella Cheese,

6 anchovy fillets

Olive Oil

Salt and Oregano

Basil

DIRECTIONS

1. Preheat the oven to 220°C (430°F).
2. Roll out the pizza dough on a pizza stone or baking sheet.
3. Spread tomato sauce over the dough.
4. Sprinkle with mozzarella cheese, olive oil, salt, and oregano.
5. Bake in the preheated oven for about 12-15 minutes or until golden brown and crispy.
6. 5 minutes before the end of cooking, add the anchovy fillets
7. Final Touches: a. Immediately top the hot pizza with fresh basil leaves.
8. Drizzle a bit more olive oil over the top if desired.
9. Slice and serve immediately.

Pizza 4 stagioni

Four Seasons Pizza

SERVINGS: 1   PREPPING TIME: 15 MIN   COOKING TIME: 12 MIN

INGREDIENTS

1 Pizza Dough

200g Tomato Sauce

100g Mozzarella Cheese, shredded

50g Artichokes, quartered

50g Ham, sliced

50g Mushrooms, sliced

50g Black Olives, sliced

Olive Oil

Salt and Oregano, to taste

DIRECTIONS

1. Preheat the oven to 220°C (430°F).
2. Roll out the pizza dough on a pizza stone or baking sheet.
3. Spread tomato sauce over the dough.
4. Divide the pizza into four quadrants. In each quadrant, place one of the toppings: artichokes, ham, mushrooms, or olives.
5. Sprinkle with mozzarella cheese, olive oil, salt, and oregano.
6. Bake in the preheated oven for about 12-15 minutes or until golden brown and crispy.

Pizza con le verdure

Vegetable Pizza

SERVINGS: 1   PREPPING TIME: 15 MIN   COOKING TIME: 12 MIN

INGREDIENTS

1 Pizza Dough
200g Tomato Sauce
100g Mozzarella Cheese, shredded
Assorted Vegetables (e.g., bell peppers, zucchini, cherry tomatoes), sliced
Olive Oil
Salt and Oregano, to taste

DIRECTIONS

1. Preheat oven to 220°C (430°F).
2. Roll out the pizza dough on a pizza stone or baking sheet.
3. Spread tomato sauce over the dough and sprinkle with mozzarella cheese.
4. Arrange the assorted sliced vegetables over the pizza.
5. Drizzle with olive oil, and season with salt and oregano.
6. Bake in the preheated oven for about 12-15 minutes or until golden and crispy.

Pizza Funghi e Salsiccia

Mushroom and Sausage Pizza

SERVINGS: 1   PREPPING TIME: 5 MIN   COOKING TIME: 12 MIN

INGREDIENTS

1 Pizza Dough

200g Tomato Sauce

100g Mozzarella Cheese, shredded

100g Mushrooms, sliced

100g Italian Sausage, crumbled

Olive Oil

Salt and Oregano, to taste

DIRECTIONS

1. Preheat the oven to 220°C (430°F).
2. Roll out the pizza dough on a pizza stone or baking sheet.
3. Spread tomato sauce over the dough and sprinkle with mozzarella cheese.
4. Distribute the sliced mushrooms and crumbled sausage evenly over the pizza.
5. Drizzle with olive oil, and season with salt and oregano.
6. Bake in the preheated oven for about 12-15 minutes until golden and crispy.

Pizza Quattro Formaggi

Four Cheese Pizza

SERVINGS: 1   PREPPING TIME: 5 MIN   COOKING TIME: 12 MIN

INGREDIENTS

1 Pizza Dough

50g Mozzarella Cheese, shredded

50g Gorgonzola Cheese, crumbled

50g Fontina Cheese, shredded

50g Parmesan Cheese, grated

Olive Oil

Oregano, to taste

DIRECTIONS

1. Preheat the oven to 220°C (430°F).
2. Roll out the pizza dough on a pizza stone or baking sheet.
3. Evenly distribute the four different cheeses over the pizza dough.
4. Drizzle with olive oil and sprinkle with oregano.
5. Bake in the preheated oven for about 12-15 minutes or until the crust is golden brown and the cheese is melted and bubbly.

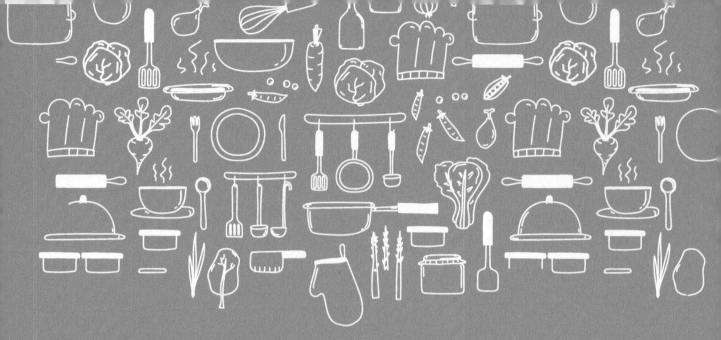

Contorni

Side Dishes

Insalata di pollo

Chicken Salad

SERVINGS: 2   PREPPING TIME: 15 MIN   COOKING TIME: 30 MIN

INGREDIENTS

300g Cooked Chicken, shredded

2 Celery Stalks, sliced

1 Red Bell Pepper, diced

100g Mayonnaise

Salt and Pepper, to taste

Fresh Parsley, chopped

Lettuce Leaves, for serving

DIRECTIONS

1. In a bowl, mix together the shredded chicken, celery, and red bell pepper.
2. Add mayonnaise, salt, pepper, and fresh parsley. Mix well.
3. Serve the chicken salad on lettuce leaves.

Frittelle Croccanti di Patate

Crispy Potato Fritters

SERVINGS: 4   PREPPING TIME: 15 MIN   COOKING TIME: 3-4 MIN

INGREDIENTS

500g Potatoes, peeled and
grated
1 Egg
50g Flour
Salt and Pepper, to taste
Vegetable oil, for frying

DIRECTIONS

1. Squeeze out excess moisture from the grated potatoes.
2. In a bowl, mix together the potatoes, egg, flour, salt, and pepper.
3. Heat oil in a frying pan and drop spoonfuls of the potato mixture into the pan.
4. Fry until golden brown on both sides, then drain on paper towels.

Polpette di Zucchine

Zucchini Meatballs

SERVINGS: 2   PREPPING TIME: 15 MIN   COOKING TIME: 30 MIN

INGREDIENTS

2 Zucchinis, grated

1 Egg

100g Breadcrumbs

50g Parmesan Cheese,
grated

Salt and Pepper, to taste

Olive Oil, for frying

DIRECTIONS

1. Squeeze excess moisture from the grated zucchinis.
2. In a bowl, combine zucchinis, egg, breadcrumbs, parmesan, salt, and pepper.
3. Form the mixture into small balls.
4. Heat olive oil in a pan and fry the meatballs until golden brown on all sides.
5. Serve warm.

Melanzane a Funghetto

Sautéed Eggplant

SERVINGS: 2   PREPPING TIME: 15 MIN   COOKING TIME: 20 MIN

INGREDIENTS

2 large eggplants

2 garlic cloves, peeled and minced

Olive oil

Salt and pepper, to taste

Fresh basil leaves, chopped

Canned peeled tomatoes (optional)

DIRECTIONS

1. Cut the eggplants into cubes and place them in a colander with salt for about 30 minutes to drain excess moisture.
2. Rinse and dry the eggplant cubes.
3. In a large pan, sauté the minced garlic in olive oil, then add the eggplant cubes.
4. Cook over medium-high heat until the eggplants are golden brown.
5. If desired, you can add canned peeled tomatoes and cook for an additional 10 minutes.
6. Season with salt and pepper, and garnish with chopped fresh basil leaves.

Cotolette di Melanzane

Eggplant Cutlets

SERVINGS: 2   PREPPING TIME: 15 MIN   COOKING TIME:5 MIN

INGREDIENTS

2 large Eggplants (sliced)

1 cup Breadcrumbs

1/2 cup Grated Parmesan
Cheese

2 Eggs (beaten)

Salt and Pepper, to taste

Olive Oil, for frying

Fresh Basil, for garnish

DIRECTIONS

1. Season the eggplant slices with salt and pepper.
2. Dip each slice in beaten eggs, then coat with a mixture of breadcrumbs and Parmesan.
3. Heat olive oil in a pan and fry the eggplant slices until golden brown on each side.
4. Drain on paper towels and garnish with fresh basil before serving.

Carciofi Fritti

Fried Artichokes

SERVINGS: 2   PREPPING TIME: 20 MIN   COOKING TIME: 10 MIN

INGREDIENTS

4 Artichokes (as desired)

Lemon Juice (to prevent browning)

Flour (for dredging)

Salt (to taste)

Oil (for frying)

DIRECTIONS

1. Clean and trim the artichokes, then cut them into slices or wedges.
2. Drizzle artichokes with lemon juice to prevent browning.
3. Dredge the artichoke pieces in flour, shaking off the excess.
4. Heat oil in a pan and fry the artichokes until golden and crispy.
5. Drain on paper towels and season with salt. Serve immediately.

Verdure Spadellate in Agrodolce

Vegetables in Sweet and Sour Sauce

SERVINGS: 4   PREPPING TIME: 20 MIN   COOKING TIME: 10 MIN

INGREDIENTS

400g Ready-made
Tomato Pulp
1 cup Vinegar
Basil, to taste
1/2 Onion
1 Eggplant
Extra Virgin Olive Oil, to
taste
2 Bell Peppers
400g Fine Peas
Salt, to taste
1 tablespoon Sugar

DIRECTIONS

1. Wash and cut all vegetables into bite-sized pieces.

2. In a pan, sauté chopped onion in olive oil until translucent, then add cubed eggplant until golden.

3. Add bell peppers and peas to the pan and cook until tender, stirring occasionally.

4. Prepare a sauce by dissolving sugar in vinegar and pour it over the vegetables.

5. Incorporate ready-made tomato pulp into the pan and combine well.

6. Season the mixture with salt and basil to taste.

7. Let it simmer until all the flavors meld together and the vegetables are cooked to preference.

8. Once the sauce has thickened, remove the pan from heat.

9. Serve the sautéed vegetables warm, optionally garnished with additional fresh basil.

Hummus di Carote e Borlotti

Borlotti Bean and Carrot Hummus Recipe

SERVINGS: 4   **PREPPING TIME: 20 MIN**   **COOKING TIME: 30 MIN**

INGREDIENTS

400g Borlotti beans, cooked and drained

2 large carrots, peeled and chopped

2 garlic cloves, peeled

2 tbsp tahini (sesame seed paste)

Juice of 1 lemon

3 tbsp extra virgin olive oil, plus extra for drizzling

Salt and pepper, to taste

Fresh parsley or coriander, for garnish (optional)

DIRECTIONS

1. Boil and cook chopped carrots until tender, then drain and set aside to cool.

2. In a food processor, combine the cooked carrots, Borlotti beans, garlic, tahini, and lemon juice.

3. Blend the mixture until smooth, adding olive oil gradually.

4. Adjust the consistency by adding water if needed.

5. Season the hummus with salt and pepper to taste.

6. Transfer the hummus to a serving bowl.

7. Drizzle with additional olive oil for garnish.

8. Optionally, garnish with fresh parsley, coriander, or a sprinkle of paprika.

9. Serve the hummus with pita bread, crackers, or fresh vegetable sticks.

Carciofi e Patate

Artichokes and Potatoes

SERVINGS: 4   PREPPING TIME: 15 MIN   COOKING TIME: 45 MIN

INGREDIENTS

4 Artichokes, cleaned and
quartered
4 Potatoes, peeled and
cubed
Olive oil
Salt and Pepper, to taste
Fresh Parsley, chopped
(optional)

DIRECTIONS

1. In a large pan, heat olive oil and sauté the artichokes and potatoes until golden.
2. Season with salt and pepper, cover, and cook until both are tender.
3. Garnish with fresh parsley if desired and serve warm.

Cotolette di Finocchi

Fennel Cutlets

SERVINGS: 2   PREPPING TIME: 15 MIN   COOKING TIME: 30 MIN

INGREDIENTS

2 Fennel Bulbs, sliced

100g Breadcrumbs

50g Parmesan Cheese, grated

2 Eggs, beaten

Salt and Pepper, to taste

Olive oil, for frying

DIRECTIONS

1. Boil the fennel slices until tender. Drain and set aside.
2. Mix breadcrumbs and parmesan in one bowl, and have beaten eggs in another.
3. Dip each fennel slice in egg, then in the breadcrumb mixture.
4. In a pan, heat olive oil and fry the fennel slices until golden brown on both sides.
5. Drain on paper towels and serve warm.

Insalata di Pollo e Avocado

Chicken and Avocado Salad

SERVINGS: 2   PREPPING TIME: 20 MIN   COOKING TIME: 20 MIN

INGREDIENTS

2 cooked Chicken
Breasts, sliced
2 ripe Avocados, diced
Mixed Salad Greens
Cherry Tomatoes, halved
Olive oil
Lemon juice
Salt and Pepper, to taste

DIRECTIONS

1. In a large bowl, combine chicken, avocados, salad greens, and cherry tomatoes.
2. In a small bowl, whisk together olive oil, lemon juice, salt, and pepper to make the dressing.
3. Drizzle the dressing over the salad, toss gently to combine, and serve immediately.

Cavolfiore alla Pizzaiola

Cauliflower Pizzaiola

SERVINGS: 2   PREPPING TIME: 15 MIN   COOKING TIME: 35 MIN

INGREDIENTS

1 Cauliflower, cut into florets
400g Tomato Sauce
2 Garlic Cloves, minced
Olive oil
Salt and Pepper, to taste
Mozzarella Cheese, shredded
Fresh Basil Leaves

DIRECTIONS

1. Preheat oven to 200°C (400°F). In a baking dish, arrange the cauliflower florets.
2. In a pan, heat olive oil and sauté garlic until golden. Add tomato sauce, season with salt and pepper, and simmer for a few minutes.
3. Pour the sauce over the cauliflower, sprinkle with mozzarella cheese, and bake until the cauliflower is tender and the cheese is melted and golden.
4. Garnish with fresh basil and serve warm.

Carciofi alla Romana

Roman-Style Artichokes

SERVINGS: 2/3   PREPPING TIME: 20 MIN   COOKING TIME: 50 MIN

INGREDIENTS

6 Artichokes
1 Lemon, juiced
2 Garlic Cloves, minced
Fresh Parsley, chopped
Olive oil
Salt and Pepper, to taste

DIRECTIONS

1. Clean the artichokes by removing the outer leaves and trimming the stems and tops.
2. Open the leaves slightly and fill with a mixture of garlic, parsley, salt, and pepper.
3. Place the artichokes in a pot, drizzle with olive oil and lemon juice.
4. Cover and cook over low heat until the artichokes are tender.

Carote lesse con aceto

Boiled Carrots with Balsamic Vinegar

SERVINGS: 2   PREPPING TIME: 10 MIN   COOKING TIME: 25 MIN

INGREDIENTS

300 g Carrots, peeled and
sliced
Balsamic Vinegar
Olive Oil
Salt and Pepper

DIRECTIONS

1. Boil carrots until tender, then drain.
2. Drizzle with balsamic vinegar and olive oil,
   season with salt and pepper.

Finocchi Gratinati

Baked Fennel

SERVINGS: 2   PREPPING TIME: 15 MIN   COOKING TIME: 30 MIN

INGREDIENTS

Fennel Bulbs, sliced

Breadcrumbs

Grated Parmesan Cheese

Olive Oil

Salt and Pepper

DIRECTIONS

1. Preheat the oven to 180°C (350°F).
2. Arrange the fennel slices in a baking dish.
3. Sprinkle with breadcrumbs, Parmesan, salt, and pepper.
4. Drizzle with olive oil and bake until golden and tender.

Peperoni al Forno

Baked Bell Peppers

SERVINGS: 2   PREPPING TIME: 15 MIN   COOKING TIME: 30 MIN

INGREDIENTS

Bell Peppers, halved and seeded

Olive Oil

Salt and Pepper

Fresh Herbs (e.g. thyme, oregano)

DIRECTIONS

1. Preheat the oven to 200°C (400°F).
2. Place the bell peppers on a baking tray, drizzle with olive oil, and season with salt, pepper, and herbs.
3. Bake until the peppers are tender and slightly charred.

Frittelle di Cipolle

Onion Fritters

SERVINGS: 2   PREPPING TIME: 15 MIN   COOKING TIME: 10 MIN

INGREDIENTS

2 large Onions, thinly
sliced

1 cup All-purpose Flour

1 cup Milk

2 Eggs

Salt and Pepper

Oil for frying

DIRECTIONS

1. In a bowl, whisk together the flour, milk, eggs, salt, and pepper to make a batter.
2. Add the sliced onions to the batter and mix well.
3. Heat oil in a frying pan. Drop spoonfuls of the onion batter into the hot oil.
4. Fry until golden brown on both sides. Drain on paper towels.

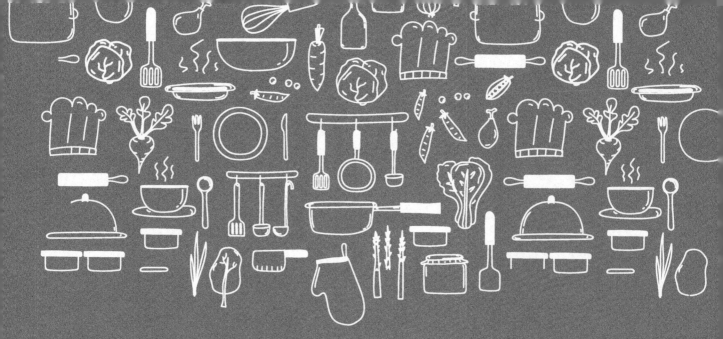

Dolce

Dessert

Biscotti al cioccolato

Chocolate Biscotti

SERVINGS: 4   PREPPING TIME:20 MIN   COOKING TIME: 20 MIN

INGREDIENTS

1 cup sugar

1 3/4 cups all-purpose flour

1/2 cup unsweetened cocoa powder

1 teaspoon baking soda

1/4 teaspoon salt

3 large eggs

1 teaspoon vanilla extract

1 cup almonds, chopped

DIRECTIONS

1. Preheat oven to 350°F (180°C). Line a baking sheet with parchment paper.
2. In a bowl, mix together sugar, flour, cocoa powder, baking soda, and salt.
3. In another bowl, whisk together eggs and vanilla. Add the wet ingredients to the dry and mix until combined. Fold in chopped almonds.
4. Form two logs on the baking sheet and bake for 35 minutes. Allow to cool for 10 minutes, then slice into 1/2-inch pieces.
5. Bake slices for an additional 10 minutes on each side. Let them cool before serving.

Sorbetto al limone

Lemon Sorbet

SERVINGS: 4   PREPPING TIME:30 MIN   COOKING TIME: NO

INGREDIENTS

170g granulated sugar

1 cup water

1 cup fresh lemon juice

1 tablespoon lemon zest

DIRECTIONS

1. In a saucepan, dissolve sugar in water over medium heat. Once dissolved, remove from heat and cool.
2. Mix in lemon juice and zest. Freeze in an ice cream maker according to manufacturer's instructions.

Ricotta Cheesecake

Ricotta Cheesecake

SERVINGS: 4   PREPPING TIME: 60 MIN   COOKING TIME: NO

INGREDIENTS

2 cups ricotta cheese

1 cup granulated sugar

1 teaspoon vanilla extract

4 large eggs

1 tablespoon lemon zest

1/4 cup all-purpose flour

1/4 teaspoon salt

DIRECTIONS

1. Preheat oven to 350°F (180°C). Grease a 9-inch springform pan.
2. In a bowl, mix ricotta, sugar, and vanilla. Add eggs one at a time, mixing well after each addition. Add lemon zest, flour, and salt, mixing just until combined.
3. Pour the mixture into the prepared pan and bake for 1 hour. Cool in the oven with the door ajar.
4. Refrigerate for at least 4 hours before serving.

Crème Brûlée

Burnt Cream

SERVINGS: 4   PREPPING TIME:30 MIN   COOKING TIME: NO

INGREDIENTS

2 cups heavy cream

1 vanilla bean, split and scraped

5 large egg yolks

1/2 cup granulated sugar, plus extra for topping

Hot water

DIRECTIONS

1. Preheat oven to 325°F (165°C) and place 4 ramekins on a baking sheet.
2. Heat Cream & Vanilla:Simmer cream with vanilla bean and pulp on medium heat, then let sit.
3. Prepare Egg Mixture: Whisk egg yolks and sugar. Gradually add cream mixture, strain for smoothness.
4. Fill Ramekins:Pour the custard mixture into the ramekins.
5. Bake: Add hot water to the baking sheet, bake for 45 mins until set but slightly wobbly.
6. Cool to room temperature, refrigerate for at least 2 hours.
7. Caramelize Sugar Topping: Sprinkle sugar on top, use a torch to caramelize, and let it harden before serving.

Tiramisù

Tiramisu

SERVINGS: 6   PREPPING TIME: 40 MIN   COOKING TIME: NO

INGREDIENTS

6 eggs

500g of mascarpone

100g of sugar

Espresso coffee, as needed

Ladyfingers (Savoiardi biscuits), as needed

Cocoa powder

DIRECTIONS

1. Separate the egg yolks from the whites. Whip the egg whites until stiff.
2. Beat the yolks with the sugar, add the mascarpone, and finally fold in the whipped egg whites.
3. Dip the ladyfingers in the coffee and arrange them in a container.
4. Alternate layers of ladyfingers and cream, ending with the cream.
5. Sprinkle with cocoa powder and let it rest in the fridge for at least 4 hours before serving.

Panna cotta

Shortcrust Pastry

SERVINGS: 4   PREPPING TIME:60 MIN   COOKING TIME: NO

INGREDIENTS

32 cups heavy cream
1 cup whole milk
1/2 cup granulated sugar
1 tablespoon vanilla
extract
2 1/4 teaspoons gelatin
powder
3 tablespoons cold water

DIRECTIONS

1. In a saucepan, combine cream, milk, sugar, and vanilla. Heat over medium heat until sugar dissolves.
2. In a small bowl, sprinkle gelatin over cold water and let it sit for 5 minutes.
3. Add gelatin to the cream mixture and stir until gelatin is completely dissolved.
4. Pour the mixture into dessert molds and refrigerate for at least 4 hours, or until firm.

Ciambellone al limone

Lemon Ciambellone

SERVINGS: 4   PREPPING TIME: 15 MIN   COOKING TIME: 30 MIN

INGREDIENTS

3 Eggs

200g Sugar

300g All-Purpose Flour

Zest and Juice of 1 Lemon

100ml Vegetable Oil

1 packet Baking Powder

Powdered Sugar, for
dusting

DIRECTIONS

1. Preheat oven to 180°C (350°F) and grease a ciambellone mold.
2. In a bowl, beat eggs with sugar until light and fluffy.
3. Add lemon zest, juice, oil, and sifted flour with baking powder.
4. Pour batter into the mold and bake for about 30-35 minutes.
5. Cool, unmold, and dust with powdered sugar.

Ciambellone carote e Mandorla

Carrot and Almond Ciambellone

SERVINGS: 4   **PREPPING TIME: 15 MIN**   **COOKING TIME: 35 MIN**

INGREDIENTS

3 Eggs

200g Sugar

200g Carrots, grated

100g Almonds, ground

200g All-Purpose Flour

100ml Vegetable Oil

1 packet Baking Powder

Powdered Sugar, for dusting

DIRECTIONS

1. Preheat oven to 180°C (350°F) and grease a ciambellone mold.
2. Beat eggs with sugar, then add grated carrots, ground almonds, oil, and sifted flour with baking powder.
3. Pour the mixture into the mold and bake for about 35-40 minutes.
4. Cool, unmold, and dust with powdered sugar before serving.

Crostata di Albicocche

Apricot Tart

SERVINGS: 4   PREPPING TIME: 15 MIN   COOKING TIME: 30 MIN

INGREDIENTS

1 Shortcrust pastry
dough
400g Apricot jam or
fresh apricots, sliced
200g Sugar (if using fresh
apricots)
1 Egg (for egg wash,
optional)

DIRECTIONS

1. Preheat the oven to 180°C (350°F).
2. Roll out the pastry dough and line a tart tin with it.
3. Spread the apricot jam evenly over the pastry or arrange fresh apricot slices and sprinkle with sugar.
4. If desired, use remaining dough to create a lattice on top and brush with beaten egg for a golden finish.
5. Bake for about 30 minutes or until the crust is golden. Let cool before serving.

Muffin al Cioccolato e Cocco

Chocolate and Coconut Muffins

SERVINGS: 4/6   PREPPING TIME: 15 MIN   COOKING TIME: 20 MIN

INGREDIENTS

200g All-purpose Flour

50g Unsweetened Cocoa Powder

150g Sugar

100g Shredded Coconut

2 tsp Baking Powder

1/2 tsp Salt

240ml Milk

90ml Vegetable Oil

2 Eggs

1 tsp Vanilla Extract

DIRECTIONS

1. Preheat the oven to 180°C (350°F) and line a muffin tin with paper liners.
2. In a bowl, sift together the flour, cocoa powder, baking powder, and salt.
3. In another bowl, whisk together the milk, oil, eggs, and vanilla extract.
4. Gradually add the wet ingredients to the dry ingredients, mixing until just combined.
5. Fold in the shredded coconut and sugar.
6. Spoon the batter into the prepared muffin tin.
7. Bake for about 20-25 minutes or until a toothpick inserted comes out clean.
8. Allow the muffins to cool in the tin for 5 minutes, then transfer to a wire rack to cool completely.

Torta Variegata alla Ricotta e Cacao

Marbled Ricotta and Cocoa Cake

SERVINGS: 4   PREPPING TIME: 15 MIN   COOKING TIME: 40 MIN

INGREDIENTS

250g Ricotta Cheese

200g Sugar

3 Eggs

200g Flour

16g Baking Powder

30g Unsweetened Cocoa Powder

1 tsp Vanilla Extract

Zest of 1 Lemon

Pinch of Salt

DIRECTIONS

1. Preheat the oven to 180°C (350°F) and grease and flour a cake tin.
2. In a bowl, mix together the ricotta cheese and sugar until smooth.
3. Add the eggs, one at a time, mixing well after each addition.
4. Sift in the flour and baking powder, then add the vanilla extract, lemon zest, and a pinch of salt, mixing until well combined.
5. Divide the batter into two portions and mix the cocoa powder into one of them.
6. Alternately spoon the plain and cocoa batters into the prepared tin.
7. Using a knife, swirl the batters together to create a marbled effect.
8. Bake for about 35-40 minutes or until a toothpick inserted comes out clean.

Dear Friends,

Thank you for joining me on this remarkable journey through authentic Italian cuisine.

Should you be inclined to spare a few moments to share your impressions, I would be grateful if you could leave a review. Your opinions are invaluable to me, and I am eagerly anticipating the opportunity to read your unique insights. Please continue to explore my culinary books via my official Amazon page at amazon.com/author/luciaproietti.

With sincere gratitude,

Lucia

Printed in Great Britain
by Amazon

34892656R00084